General Management
for
Operational
Managers

General Management
for
Operational
Managers

Practical guidelines and answers covering
"1001" questions and situations

R<small>UDOLF</small> H<small>ARTONG</small>

authorHOUSE®

AuthorHouse™ UK Ltd.
1663 Liberty Drive
Bloomington, IN 47403 USA
www.authorhouse.co.uk
Phone: 0800.197.4150

Published by AuthorHouse 5/23/2013

ISBN: 978-1-4817-8881-6 (sc)
ISBN: 978-1-4817-9679-8 (e)

This book is printed on acid-free paper.

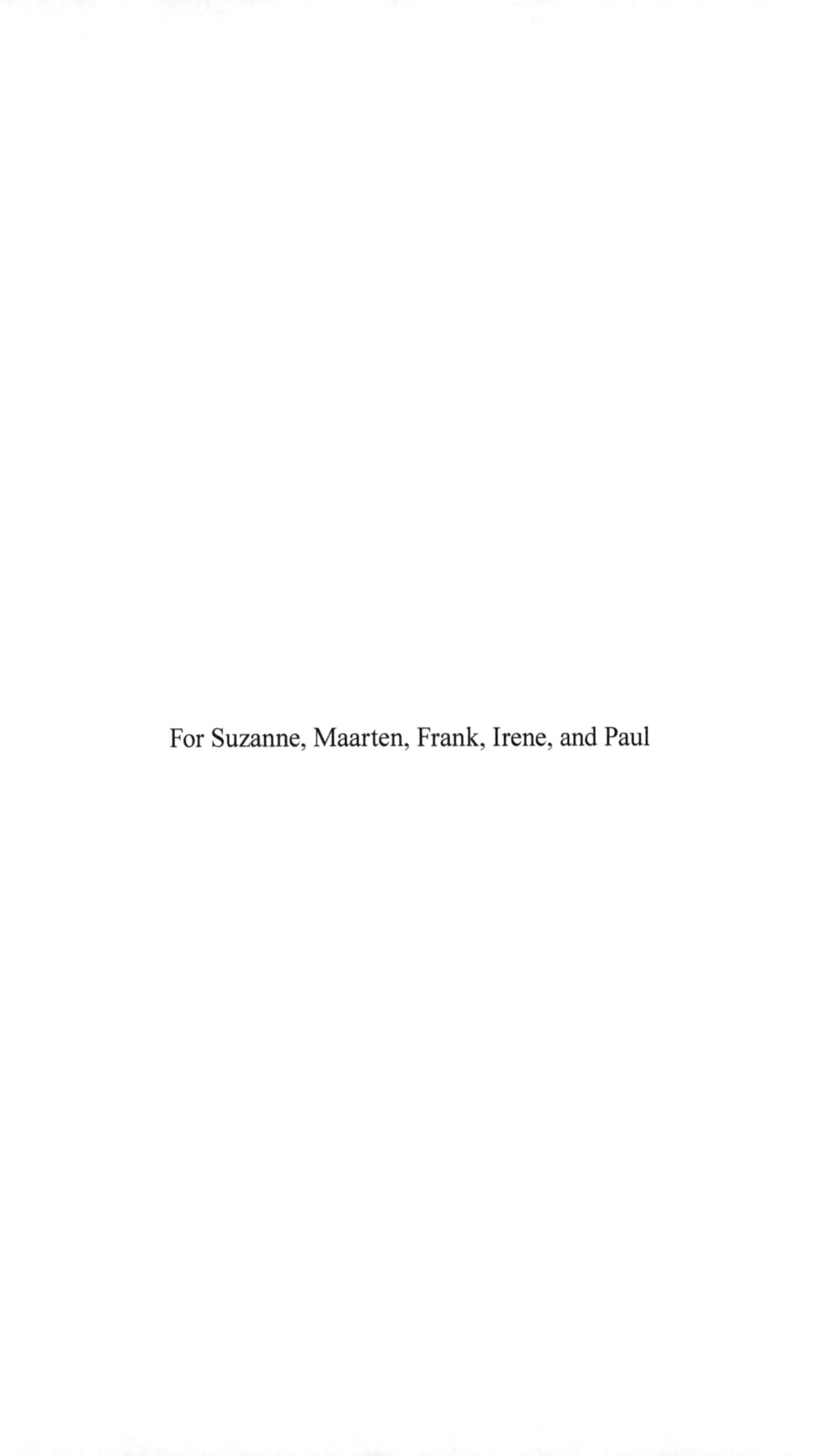

For Suzanne, Maarten, Frank, Irene, and Paul

PREFACE

This small book is neither a scientific book nor an academic study based on theories. It is a book based on a very practical approach learned over eighteen years of working in general management.

I will describe and explain general management in operational situations. I will give answers to many questions involving a variety of situations that many newly-appointed general managers will experience, or have already experienced if they manage operations. A few of the situations I will describe will begin with your need to ask yourself, *Who am I?* I will move on to discuss cultural aspects, the uniqueness of a local company, and alcohol and drug abuse. I hope that my explanations and examples will help to improve a person's management skills.

Of course, there exist general management positions within head or central offices; but these are less related to operational matters, and individuals may not encounter many of the experiences confronted by managers in operations. I certainly do not intend to disqualify their work (having worked in a head office myself). Quite to the contrary; but this book is limited to the description of my experiences in operational positions.

Why are you a general manager?

Members of your top management team may have selected you and given you this opportunity because of the following factors:

- They recognized all the hard work you did in your previous position, such as physically hard work, long hours, or many trips abroad.

- You delivered good results.

- You followed and executed the instructions and directives of top management and met their expectations.

- You managed to get a large order in on time.

There could be many reasons why you were chosen for this job. But, in any case, you now have the job of general manager, managing director, president, executive vice president, director, or whatever title comes with the position.

I am of the opinion that you were selected to be a general manager not only because of all the reasons I mentioned above but also because you used your creativity and your ability to solve problems in a non-conventional way by "thinking outside the box".

The only way to be creative is through relaxing, not by working sixty or eighty hours a week. "Work smart" is the expression, but in reality it does not mean anything. Hard work, coupled with working long hours, can be necessary from time to time. But it does not make you creative.

Occasionally, you have to relax, take a step back and give yourself feedback. You may want to ask yourself some questions such as: *What am I doing now?, Was this the right decision?, Did I treat my team member too tough in our last meeting?, A project has failed – did I support it enough?, Why did we lose that order?, How can we prevent this from happening again?, What lessons did we learn?, Did I put the right person on that job?*

The way to relax, to be able to be creative, to take a step back, is a very personal one; but you should know what is best for you. It might be to have a drink in a bar, enjoy a sport such as jogging, or go for a walk along the beach with a loved one or close friend.

In conclusion, you have to find out what works best for you, but it is essential that you know how to relax.

Unfortunately, in spite of having great careers, a lot of people do not know themselves. Really, you have to get to know yourself including all of your weak points and hidden secrets. You have to be aware of your strengths and weaknesses and handle them well. Otherwise, people might take advantage.

One important piece of advice is that you should never drink (too much) at company functions or after meetings and/or events. Remember, your behaviour will always be observed; and even if your own boss is drinking too much, you should refrain. I have seen many careers ruined because of too much alcohol. If you need an extra drink to relax, do it privately. You must know your limitations.

Knowing the Peter Principle – to be promoted beyond your level, up to the level of incompetence – is the basic condition for good leadership for a general manager. (See the note at the end of this preface.) You learn about yourself best when you are dealing with a crisis. When you are faced with a difficult situation (i.e., you are dismissed from your job, your child is seriously ill, or some other disaster in your life occurs), you find yourself confronted with yourself. It is through this difficulty that you learn how to fight and overcome crises. To know yourself comes about from not just how you deal with good experiences and successes, but also – and especially – failures in your job or in traumatic situations.

Relaxing and being creative also helps you to avoid physical illness, such as a heart attack, an ulcer, or any of the many managerial diseases that often arise after long exposure to stress. Enjoy your work! Never a dull moment!

The most important aspect of you in your position as general manager is your personality. Your bosses, employees, customers, and competitors will all be observing you, and, therefore, you must be your true self as much as possible. You are who you are and to know that is the basis of being a good general manager.

Now you can begin this challenging, fascinating and rewarding job. Your top management entrusted you with the responsibility for a company or part of a company in production, engineering, project management or sales, or even a completely integrated company with all disciplines represented. What an honour!

I have enjoyed all of this during the eighteen years I was working in general management. I helped, supported, gave directions, created solutions and coached teams in order that the company could develop into a better position. I was able to contribute to that success. It is very challenging to create solutions with companies in unique situations. No manual was, or is, available which shows a person what to do and how to do it. Every company and each country is unique and the solution to success is also unique. Success is the most motivational and rewarding element of the job, more than a bonus or other compliments.

In this book I will explain my experiences to you in the hope that you may recognize them and conclude that you were not the only one who had a good or bad feeling or experience.

Being a general manager in an operation also carries with it an element of isolation. You stand alone in difficult decisions during which, your personality (who you are) will help you. This book will give you some advice and insight as to how I handled difficult and different situations. That does not mean that my handling was always good or correct, but you can think about it and form your own opinions and possibly learn from it.

Rudolf Hartong

May 2013

Note: The Peter Principle states that members of a hierarchy are promoted until reaching a level at which they are incompetent. This describes people who were good and excelled in their previous jobs but failed in new positions with more prestige, salary, and growth. Promotion is not always a good thing for a person or for the related company. In short, it illustrates how being promoted and rewarded with a higher position may eventually cause one to exceed his or her field of expertise.

ACKNOWLEDGEMENTS

I would like to thank very much Ilias Aliev, Ton Coenen, Annette Dill-Andree, Cameron Skandarioon, Jean-Louis Vuille, and my wife, Johanna, for their valuable contributions, comments, and reactions to make this book what it is now.

Frank Hartong took the picture on the cover.

TABLE OF CONTENTS

CLARIFICATION: GENERAL MANAGEMENT AND LEADERSHIP

This is a topic so well known that I have to address it and give you my view before I explain some of the cases and situations I have encountered.

Too often these words are said: "Congratulations! As general manager, you are a leader!" What does that mean? Numerous books have been written, and new ones will be written, about management and leadership. Sometimes these concepts are mixed up and not very understandable. Often management is described as activities concentrating on (financial) administrative procedures, organization (human resources), growth (sales) and products (development). For example, it means having the (financial) books in order, the procedures followed up and keeping the company running in the way that it should. That is not an easy job!

Leadership has to do with vision, drive, and passion. But a company cannot be run by leadership alone. It needs the solid base of a functioning management. Leadership can make a breakthrough and steer a company into a new direction on a new and successful path.

Who are leaders? Churchill and de Gaulle are often mentioned as leaders during the Second World War. Entrepreneurs, such as Steve Jobs and Bill Gates are often called leaders, starting up complete new industries by their inventions. They call the Pope the leader of a church. You can be leader of a family or tribe. "Leaders are born," as the saying goes. Others say that leaders are made by circumstances and the time in which they live. A leader does not need to be a famous person or a CEO of a company. He or she can also be a manager of a small company or organization. I became a manager and acted sometimes as a leader based on my skills, which I learned in earlier experiences through giving feedback to myself, observing my managers and leaders, developing a vision, and, of course, from making mistakes. Also, management training and education helped because it gave me the opportunity to reflect on my own behaviour; but it was not the main factor. It was the ambition, conviction, self-learning and vision which made me a manager and leader, as was told to me by my employees.

Leaders are called leaders afterwards because of what they did or achieved. Compare this with company culture as being the unwritten process of actions and activities which makes a company unique. Afterwards and after many years of successes, people start writing it down. Such people, often called entrepreneurs, do things differently! Leaders are called leaders by the people, by the employees, never by the person himself or herself, or by the Board or the top management. If that were to happen, it then becomes a fashion trend and has nothing to do with real leaders.

In management there are definitely elements of leadership needed. Depending on the situation, these leadership elements come more to the surface than in other situations such as, in case of a strike, big claims, catastrophes, new product development activities, expanding or downsizing of companies and workforce. So, for me, management and leadership are linked. Sometimes you act more as manager, the next time more as leader when the situation requires you to do so.

In conclusion, a manager is a person who manages, but who also needs to have leadership capabilities within him- or herself such as vision, drive and passion. Time and situation decide your role.

I heard a CEO just recently on TV make the comment "Leadership happens or shows when you are not there!" If you have put your organization in order and in the right direction, it will also function well when you are not present.

I paraphrase Colin Powell: when your people stop coming to you with their problems, you are not their leader anymore.

SECTION 1 –
"1001" QUESTIONS ABOUT
GENERAL MANAGEMENT

1.0 How do you start as a general manager in an operation or company?

- The first day is important because your employees will observe you. They will compare you with their former boss. How do you want to make an impact and show that a new manager has arrived? Do you want to change your office or your car? In a company that is financially in a difficult situation, it is not wise to spend a lot of money on the new boss's "hobbies" as your employees will see it. You should, however, implement some changes to make your point that a new general manager has arrived. Introduce yourself to all employees, be visible, "walk the talk", make changes in respect to the ideas or vision you have in order to show the areas where you will put emphasis. For instance, if your emphasis will be on quality, visit the quality control department; or, perhaps it's to give extra attention to sales or production.

- I remember a situation, having started as the new general manager, where I made comments about the rather dirty situation in the production hall and locker rooms and asked for it to be cleaned up. When my request was not followed up, I took a broom and did it myself! That helped.

- Realize that each company is unique and has its own specified culture, based on the history of that company and the cultural environment. Spend time in understanding that because it will help a lot in preparing your plans. There is no ready-made manual for you.

- Take time and pay attention to the managers who are already in place. It is of great importance to understand them and to know how they see their job, how they interact with their employees, and to know their personal ambitions and goals. It can help in selecting the people you want to keep and who you can trust, and determining if they share your way of doing business.

- Make yourself familiar with the organization, your management team and all staff. I mean *all*. Even if you have 1000 employees, meet all of them. When you are visible, people will be able to contact you and talk with you about their problems. You will hear a lot and it is good that your managers will see this so they will work to avoid a complaint the next time and treat people correctly (if that was not the case before). Support your managers, but you need to bear in mind that in some cases, some staff may be under the influence of the local management team that has its own agenda and does not hesitate to put people under pressure to resist a new general manager's efforts toward change. This pattern does not support the company and creates a bad atmosphere; therefore, you must break it! In this book I will give advice and examples on how best to do that.

- If you have a language problem, and do not speak the local language fluently, you can learn a great deal from their body language. In addition, nowadays there are always people around who can speak some English.

- Get yourself introduced to all the committees which exist in the company such as, health and safety, works council, canteen, quality and claim committee, to mention a few.

- Focus on quality in general. What is the quality situation of the company? What about the number of claims? How many production and/or engineering mistakes (non-conformity reports) are being logged? What is the level of returned goods? After a while, plan customer and supplier visits. Discuss quality issues with them in order to gain a good insight.

- Visit all your main customers and suppliers. Both are important. Take care that you are introduced to all visitors as well as new and future customers. If visitors, for example, are new customers, ensure they are guided around the company, and be part of the tour. It shows your commitment and interest not just to the customer, but also to your employees. Be visible.

- Get introduced to all newly-employed staff. As time

goes by, ensure that you are a part of, or at least follow, the selection procedures. Work together with your HR department, because it is of eminent importance that you get the right persons in the right jobs.

- It all looks like a lot to control; but this is what you need to do in the beginning. Ask your staff to report all details to you on a daily basis. This will help you to get a quick overview of the procedures and a clear view of what is taking place. Later, if you get the feeling that it could work, you can always change this procedure by delegating the responsibility back to the relevant persons in charge.

- Contact, or involve yourself, in the external contacts/relations with government, municipalities and, if posted abroad, the embassy, to mention a few. This will aid you in knowing how your company is viewed by outsiders. Develop a kind of "antenna" to follow how people think about you and your company from time to time. As well, you need to get a feeling as to what your bosses think about you and the way you manage the staff and the company.

Take the time to understand all departments in your company. No department is better or more important than any other. They cannot perform without the other. But, in my opinion, there are two important fundamental issues that are basic to the running of all other departments, including finance, sales, production and HR, to mention a few. Without a good financial set up, the company will not work well; and without good, well-trained staff, you will not get anywhere.

1.1   How do you settle in as a family?

A new position often means moving to another house or apartment, a new town or even country. Sometimes you take up a job far away from your home country as an expatriate. The children need a new school, your family a new home. Everybody in your family is excited but also, a little nervous about how everything will work out. Saying goodbye to good friends and family members who stay behind is not easy.

In our family we had developed a pattern. Our family knew when the contract would end, so when the end of an assignment approached, they began asking questions. Would the contract be prolonged or do we prepare for the next move? When our children grew up, we had a meeting around the table to discuss an eventual next move and related job offer. Whenever possible, together we planned a visit to the new city or country and eventually school(s). In that way, the children and my partner were able to form an opinion.

It helps to discuss the new offer and decide on it together as a family. The company's human resources department can be of great help by taking away some worries. Language courses, if needed, can start beforehand; and sometimes a course about the culture of the new country is not a waste of money. For our family, the schools were the first item to settle. After that we tried to find a home in the same neighbourhood as the school(s). My workplace, and its distance from our home, was the last thing we worried about.

It's prudent to first take care that the family gets settled in the best possible way and is happy. That will avoid a lot of problems later on. If you have to drive a little longer to your workplace (for instance, one hour), just accept that.

It is helpful if you can start to work a few months early in your newly-assigned workplace. In this way, you have time to prepare for your family's needs, get the house ready and then you can concentrate 100% on your new job. When your family arrives, most of the urgent details are settled. Again, your HR department can help here with visas, permits, etc. that may be required.

In my next book, *What Changed Our Lives*, I will go into more depth regarding what's involved in moving around.

1.2   How do you handle the takeover period?

Everybody is different and does things his or her way, but I always preferred to have the takeover period between me and my predecessor as short as possible at just one week, or a maximum of two weeks. Nothing against my predecessors – it's not that I would disagree with the way they did their jobs. On the contrary! But you will want to do it your way and be independent and free as soon as possible. In this one- or two-week period, your predecessor can brief you about all the eventual problems and situations he or she is currently facing as well as inform you about historical issues that are relevant for you. If you have a long takeover period, it is possible that you or your predecessor might get irritated, which could become a hindrance for you in getting started the way you want. Normally, you can always call or contact your predecessor about specific items you discover later on such as agreements or contracts.

1.3   Preparation of a business plan

After two to three months in the new job, it is time to prepare, along with your management team, a plan of activities and initiatives that you and your team want to take to improve certain weak elements in the company. Let each department manager prepare a short paper with their aims and goals for their department. It is helpful if they use a SWOT (Strengths, Weaknesses, Opportunities and Threats) analysis of their department. All these reports can help you and serve as a basis for an overall business plan. There are many examples of a business plan that can be found on the Internet. There is also plenty of literature available on this subject. As well, there should be business plan examples available in your company's head office, which can guide you on how to prepare and produce such a plan. If a big reorganization is needed due to financial reasons, lack of sales, quality awareness actions, or any action needed to "turn the ship around", then you must act as leader because you cannot expect that your management team will drive this. That means that most of the business plan will need to be written by you, since you have the vision and experience to be able to "turn the ship around".

Here is an example of a condensed version of a business plan:

- Mission Statement (critical success factors, strategy, organization)

- Future of the company (niche?)

- Forecasts and income contributors

- Organizational development

- Adjustment of workforce

- Budget estimations and proposals

- Investments for restructuring costs

- Summary

1.4   Employee representatives

A works council or other employee representatives are important. Ask them to make a list of what they think is important in order to improve the status of the company and/or the situation for the employees. Discuss it together, and also discuss the new business plan; ask for understanding and cooperation. You will be met with hesitation because they do not yet know you, so they will be careful and keep an eye on your actions. That is a good sign because you must also understand their position and point of view. Normally, you all have the same goal: to make the company better and stronger. By achieving that, you also help the workforce with stability and a future. Discuss together your plan and their list for improvements. At least once a year, check their list with them and take care progress has been made. In this way you create trust, and you show that you are serious about dealing with some of the problems mentioned. Create deadlines for all the actions proposed and promised. This will introduce a sense of urgency into what has been agreed and what you want to achieve.

In my experience, the attitude of "care and be fair" is the best answer. If you do not show it in your actions, then it becomes a hollow phrase.

Ban politics in your company. For instance, you may notice that suggestions or plans are made which are not focussed on making the company better, and they are not targeting the main goals. Sometimes members of your management team or the works council representatives try to play politics. You need to ensure that it stops. Be open and fair, be objective, and have only the company and the development of it as the main factor upon which decisions are based. You stop the politics by ignoring them or by clearly addressing them.

1.5   Building of a local team

Building a local team is the most important task you have in front of you, especially if the company needs a turnaround or other painful operation. Your employees will already have a sense as to the nature of the situation. They may know more than you realize. They notice the lack of orders, claims, quality problems and delivery delays. They also notice what is done correctly and what needs to be improved. They have open channels of communication around the whole company and through this, can put two and two together to understand the company's situation. There are probably no secrets among them. So there you are! What are you going to do?

What I did in most cases was to gather all employees and inform them about the situation. I explained how I saw it; I asked if there were questions, and tried to get an understanding of what had to be done. I asked for their help and support. At this point, you will not get that openly because they do not know you nor trust you (yet). Trust is built on performance; but a start has been made.

Now focus on your management team. Have meetings and discuss the situation. Ask how they see the situation and get their commitment. Team building is easier said than done, but it has to do with both your personality as general manager, and that of your management team members. I always prefer to have team members from different disciplines, backgrounds and I also avoid "yes men" in my management team. Careful choices make for a diverse, vibrant and successful team as the best comes out of sometimes-heated discussions. Make some adjustments in the organization so people see something is happening. Be fair and open. Show leadership. If members of your team do not function as you feel they should, remove them or transfer them to another position. Your employees will see this and will know if it is the right decision. They will have also noticed that the person did not function well, or perhaps was using politics all the time to save his job. Therefore, in this way you will have made the first step toward gaining trust.

Discuss the company business plan with the employee representatives. Get them on board or at least gain their approval to continue. Together, with a new and re-energized management team, you can begin to get the process going. Employees will come to you (when you are visible) and give you their input and comments on what you are doing. That is a positive start. You will get a feeling of togetherness, or bonding, and slowly this is going to move things in the direction you want.

Organize sporting events, family days, company open house days and many more activities for the workforce. In that way, your team will feel that things are moving into a new dimension of which they can be proud. They will be proud to be a member of a winning team!

Invest in training and an evaluation or appraisal system for the employees. It is important for the employees to know how they perform in respect of the objectives of the company.

Celebrate any new orders. Create a communication channel, which could be just an A4 sheet of paper posted where everyone can see, or perhaps an announcement via the computer intranet system informing all employees of the successes and also claims received. Communication is crucial in this process! You, as general manager, are central to this phase toward change. At times, this is a very time-consuming and tiring process, but when you see some success, this is very encouraging, too! When you reach that phase, it is also important to change your role from leader to coach. Test your management team to see if they show initiative. Then, if you can, delegate. Your time in that company is temporary, so it is important that you build up a strong management team, which will be able to continue on their own when you leave.

1.6   Motivation

It is easy to say that you must have motivation, but it is very difficult to create and maintain. Not only your own motivation, on which you constantly need to work even when there are developments that go wrong and affect your hopes and ambitions, but also, the motivation of your team and your employees.

It might be time again for you to ask yourself *Who am I?* This brings you back to the fundamental truth of your ambitions, hopes, fears and will power; and from this process comes the answer to how to continue. It will also give you new energy to focus on the direction you are aiming to take the company.

Training can be a motivator in some circumstances. Sometimes regaining motivation is made easy with remuneration or status symbols. For some people, salary or bonuses have nothing to do with their motivation. Even if they were not paid, or had a very low salary, they would do the same job with the same enthusiasm and motivation.

What motivates you when all the signs or developments are against you, especially when you know that you are right? Having experience, conviction, vision, and determination can all be very strong motivators. People, and also your employees, see and feel your motivation, and that can give them the motivation as well to continue to fight for orders or to get the quality right. It helps having frequent discussions with your staff, "walking the talk" with them, feeling and having an intuition when the motivation is low. Then you can take steps and actions to re-energize your management team. Or, discuss the situation openly. You could ask them open questions such as, *What is going on guys? Your enthusiasm is low. What can we do about it?* Or perhaps, *Is the process or the fight to win too long? Are you getting tired?* Perhaps training can be a kind of motivation for the managers. You might ask them, *Do we have to give you new blood? Or do we have to reorganize and bring new people in?* As general manager or managing director, you certainly act as the leader; but the leader must have the direction or vision crystal clear in order for him- or herself first.

CASE ONE: HOW MOTIVATION CAN WORK AND ALSO FALL APART

I experienced a situation in a company where a very dominant and super-tough manager of a big department was very successful within his department. He experienced good sales and growth, good results and hard work from his people who had great respect for him. In spite of that, he paid rather low salaries. But he was able to keep his people together and focusing on the job in a booming economy.

This person left the company and was replaced by a "soft" manager who used completely the opposite type of management. A hole was created in leadership, and the competition took advantage of the situation. The employees felt suddenly uncomfortable. They became aware of their low salary level, which had previously not been a big issue for them. When the competitor offered them attractive salaries, they suddenly found their motivation was completely gone because their management did not act quickly. This caused not just one or two employees to leave the company, but within two months, 40% of the workforce had quit!

We had to reorganize the whole department, adjust the salaries to market level and had to work on motivation and a new strategy. In the meantime, we got help from colleagues in other countries who were able to send us staff to bridge the gap until we had built up a new team.

In conclusion, motivation can keep people together in difficult situations to a certain point (elasticity). But when the cohesion collapses, things fall apart. Therefore, my advice is, if you are confronted, as the new GM, with such a dominant, super-tough manager, you can let it go because the motivation and aspiration of that person is high. Work with the principles he or she is operating with. Interfere only when you see that overtime and hard work are stretching the workforce too much, or if you find out that the salaries are not at market level. So, support this manager, but at the same time give extra attention to his or her environment. This approach can work. Sometimes it may happen that you have conflicts and difficult discussions with him or her, but that will help the overall situation and could avoid a collapse when such a person leaves. Do not kick him or her out, because a good contribution has been made. Just follow, guide and sometimes confront to get it right.

1.7 How do you deal with your superior/boss/chairman of the board?

Most likely it would have been your superior who offered you the job. It is important to have a good and constructive relationship with him or her. You got this assignment and you have been briefed about what he or she thinks has to be done. Priorities will be mentioned. In most cases, it has to do with financial difficulties, negative results, quality problems or issues in sales and production. When you have started the new position, ensure the tasks, which you have set together with your boss, are appropriate. If not, discuss it and explain how you see it. Get the support from him or her. Ask also for their agreement of your presented business plan. After a few months in the job, invite your superior for a visit. During that visit you can discuss your business plan, as well as the progress and problems you see and the support you may need from head office. He or she can help you. Normally, a boss does not like to always hear about problems. That is why he or she has given you the job! So endeavour to solve them on your own. Be careful not to bother him or her with all kinds of local problems. You have to manage that yourself. Just follow your own ideas. Your boss will keep an eye on you and check how you do via discussions with your management team members when they visit the head office. Or your boss might use other channels to gather information. If finally the result and success is coming, you will get even more support offered. This can result in a lot of visits from many staff persons from central organizations. They want to be part of the success and give you all kinds of advice (mostly too late and of no use). Your company becomes popular. People want to take part in the success when the hard work is done. They want to "shine" also.

1.8   How to handle "good boss"/"bad boss"

Unfortunately, you are not in a position to select your superior. You can, however, have a good working relationship with your superior where you can learn a lot from him or her and get the support that you need to meet your targets. It is good to have such support, especially if you have a tough job to do. But sometimes the chemistry does not work. You or your boss get irritated, you do not get the support you need and you do not feel recognized, but put aside. I have always advised to colleagues, based on my own experience of working with a difficult boss, to act professionally, and to do their job in a good and professional way. The situation can get complicated, especially when you get a new boss in the meantime, but not necessarily, it can work well and even better.

No boss or superior, even if he or she does not seem to appreciate you as a person, can deny it when you do a good job and that the results you deliver are good too. Doing a good job can be a saving grace and will close the door on a lot of interference from the top. In such cases, you must try to avoid too much contact by keeping to only the most essential contact, such as during budget reviews; and then, you must ensure the details are prepared to the standards expected by your superior. It can happen that your boss will get a promotion or another assignment, and the problem is solved by itself. Or you could finish your contract and prepare for a new assignment based on the good results you and your team achieved. In some situations, you should look for another position outside the company; but bear in mind, you could also encounter the same sort of difficult situation again. Being a professional in your work will help you a lot. Nobody can deny that.

Sometimes you have to deal with a lot of politics. The organization may be split into camps. Your boss, for example, may be a personal friend of the CEO. You are not; and therefore, it can happen that you are forced to make a choice, in favour or against. This may be a very difficult and traumatic situation. Make your choice based on your professional competence, not on the basis of a friendly relationship with a key person belonging to one or the other camp. Should the CEO leave, some people may find themselves in a difficult situation because they lost their support. Be a professional! (Know your job as general manager.) And if you are not a professional, then make every effort to become one or you are lost, making it appear that the boss you did not get on with was right.

1.9   Do you need to focus on your own and your company's public relations?

Your own PR, your image in the company, is very important, especially if you are based in a country far away from head office. You may be in a country that does not play a major role in your company. In this case, you become very easily isolated and do not get the information and gossip from central or head office. You need to develop communication that relies on friends or your boss, if he or she supports you.

It is very important that you are not forgotten, especially when you are in need of another assignment or the end of your contract approaches. If you can get articles in the company newsletter, or the company is mentioned in another way for example because of its good products, high quality, or successful turnaround, then this gives your profile a boost and will definitely help your career. Good PR is also important for the company you manage. It will make your people proud and helps with motivation, creating a good atmosphere. So make sure you give some time and attention to PR. However, do not act as a "showmaster" because this will work against you; act in a professional way. Let the company and your people be your best PR instrument. There is a fine line between working on PR without calling too much attention to you as general manager. In my opinion, you should fight for your company and your employees when necessary. Then it is you who takes the PR role and when the objective is achieved, you withdraw and let the company and its employees continue.

1.10 Is support needed for staff functions from head office?

Of course! Professional and specialist support is always welcome and appreciated, though, not in the following case:

During an assignment, I noticed a lot of people from the head office visiting our location on their own initiative, meaning, without an invitation. While there, they pretended to give support and advice. They spent a lot of time in meetings and discussions and gave orders as to what our staff should be doing. Then, after a lot of dinners and entertaining, they left. Our local people were unsure how to handle that as these visitors seemed important because they came from the head office. In the local culture they could not, and would not, have acted to stop it, so they would have just let it continue. I felt I needed to intervene and stop that type of interference immediately.

I had to tell them, "You are most welcome and we appreciate your advice, but only when *we* need it and invite you, not the other way around." The reaction I received was not positive. It took them some time to understand this, during which I was not the most popular person with head office. We had to stop this sort of interference because it created a lot of work and wasted the time of the local staff. We needed to focus on the priorities we had set ourselves. By taking this action, it made my position clear in the company I had been hired to manage. Our employees knew which side I was on and that helped me a lot.

Good and competent support is always welcome and needed. Often, you miss that in an organization which is in trouble. But you and your staff must carry on because you know the company's unique culture and how best to make changes. That must be clearly understood, even in head office, and then it will work out well. Advice can be given in the areas of engineering (new design systems), finance (control and system support), IT (system support), production (lean management, efficiency), human resources (selection, central HR policies), supply management (new central contracts, reporting), after sales and services (customer training) and sales/marketing (new channels, systems), to give some examples. Everything must be done in a planned and controlled manner.

1.11 Do we need to contract specialist help from outside?

Every company is unique, as I have often stated. Most of the problems and challenges can be best handled using your own resources, creativity and initiatives. But of course, there are cases where you need local specialists to help you. For example, in case of redundancies and other issues that may be subject to particular regulation, which differs from country to country, you need lawyers and local HR advisors working together with your local HR department.

Head offices and other central offices can provide a good amount of competent assistance. If you have a good business plan, they will be more willing to support you. Financial specialists from central office are most welcome because they can advise you in reporting and special cases (financing of the redundancy costs). Also production can make use of specialist help regarding new systems, quality systems or other introductions, which can improve efficiency. Quality control may occasionally need a revision of their quality certificates. When inspectors from specialized companies come in to perform an audit, they can, at the same time, give you new ideas on how things are organized in your company. They can also make suggestions and remarks as to whether the company is complying with the demands of the quality certificate, such as ISO (International Organization for Standardization).

But, you, as general manager, must control and coordinate this advice in a way that it is balanced and will not upset the whole company, because too many initiatives can take away focus from the important tasks you have in front of you.

CASE TWO: QUALITY COUNTS

After many difficult negotiations, we received a nice order from a Japanese customer. It was a big job, but we managed to do it right; also, it went well financially. The next project this customer had, we lost to a foreign competitor on price. This second project took a year to complete. Six months later we were called by a very worried customer because this installation had gone completely wrong! There were problems due to the bad quality of the installed equipment as well as issues with late delivery.

The customer claimed more than one million (USD) in damages from the supplier. In a meeting that followed, they asked us to take over this project and remove all the material! We accepted this challenge and made a success out of it.

This Japanese customer told us that for them, "only quality counts". In this case, being too price-oriented proved a mistake.

In conclusion, even if you have to fight on price, never ever lower your quality standards. Sometimes you lose an order, but at the other end, you get orders back. This example illustrates that.

1.12   How do you handle obstacles if you do not have the full support from your staff?

Each company has its own history which you must take the time to study. It can be filled with strikes, failures, redundancies, successes, bad communication with head office, feelings of not being well respected, inappropriate management, strained relationships with workers' representatives, and so on. So when you take up a position as the new general manager and you are already a little familiar with the company's background, you should not expect the welcome to be genuinely warm even though this is what people pretend. This is due to the historical background.

I already explained how you could start, but it is difficult to get the majority on your side and it takes time. Start with a small group, like your management team and some members of various committees.

Your management team is crucial. You have to give it a lot of attention, so the outside world sees and experiences a unified team that stands behind the actions it plans. Show your intention and take action with a few items which need urgent attention. For example, you could clean up and do some renovation of the canteen, or organize and create a better sales team by strengthening that department, take special actions related to health and safety or install a new engineering system. It all depends where the weak spots are that you have discovered. When you have done that, some people will become enthusiastic and will begin to turn in your direction to support you. You have made a start.

Slowly, taking your time, discuss the problems. Explain now that you have changed the organization of the sales department, how you expect sales will go up, or customer claims will come down. Celebrate a success, a positive change.

There will always be persons who may work against you and try to boycott your initiatives. Once you have identified them, talk to them one by one and warn them that you will not tolerate any unconstructive behaviour. Some people will understand and change, some may not. In that case, you must fight and show your leadership. I had one such case in which I did not dismiss the person. Instead I gave him a new job, a more important job, and he changed completely! He finally got the attention he deserved and became a very good contributor to the change process. In another case, I had a very clear and tough face-to-face meeting with a person in opposition who was making moves against the suggested changes. I simply told him what I expected from him and that turned out to be helpful. It is often too easy to suggest that the person be kicked out. I believe it is preferable to make the effort to fully understand a person and to make use of the skills and abilities inherent in such a person. Even if he or she is a difficult person, they may have professional experience and know-how that are invaluable to the process. Slowly you turn the company, with everyone's help, in the right direction and deliver success.

1.13 Are you always acting like an agent of change?

I would have to say the answer is: not always. A lot depends on the job and the challenges ahead of you. If the company or big department needs growth, then you have to prepare for that growth. That is very fulfilling. Everybody will be on board to get that done. Then your function is more that of a coach stimulating people to take action. You give the first indication of change by explaining and introducing a new policy or vision, strategy or direction that you want to bring to the company. If it is growth, for instance, into a new field or area of business, then your commercial people will be enthusiastic and you can delegate. But you have to oversee the process to ensure that it goes in the right direction!

If the new direction of the company forces changes related to, for instance, some of its products, organization or new reporting lines, then yes, you act as an agent of change, a turnaround manager, or re-engineering person, or whatever name is suitable. In such cases, you have to take the lead, at least in the beginning.

I began by doing research about the status (commercial and financial) of the company and the products we were producing or selling. I looked to find where the problems were. My actions were partly related to visiting and talking to customers. Then, together with a small team consisting of the financial manager, and the sales and engineering people, I analyzed the short and long term future. We made a business plan, and from there we followed through.

1.14 How do you handle redundancies?

In a situation where a company may have made many losses over many years, and the financial situation is not improving, with actions and initiatives to improve the situation having failed, something has to be done. Everybody will understand that, especially the employees, because they experience the situation every day. Action is needed to bring costs down and in balance with the newly-planned organization and company. Firstly, study the working processes within the company. Perhaps the same amount of work can be done with less people.

Everything must be based on a company business plan. If there is a good plan, and growth is foreseen in the near future, one should be careful when downsizing staff. Downsizing can cause the loss of valuable competence and expertise, which will probably be needed in the near future.

This is a valid argument, especially in emerging markets, because they normally show a growth pattern. The company can benefit from that situation after the reorganization. In addition, staff costs in emerging countries are not very high (yet), so the cost savings are limited, especially if the plan is to grow later on. In that case, I would advise being careful with a decision to reduce staff numbers.

In one country, when the order situation was bad, we took our own initiative. We called the process a "move forward" initiative (not sitting down in apathy waiting for orders, but fighting for them). We asked ourselves where we could identify a need for the products and how it would be possible to procure the orders. We involved everybody in the company, all levels of staff, including the production people. We felt that some staff may have had family members with the right contacts that could have been of help in bringing orders in to secure new sales contracts. New sales leads could then be followed. By mobilizing everybody, you grow enthusiasm, and in this case, it worked extremely well! After a few months, new orders began to come in. With this action, we limited the loss during a bad year. So, do not give in too easily when you are under pressure to cut staff numbers. Your people are the most valuable asset you have!

If this is not the answer, then you will have to try something else. Another approach might be to downsize and base the new organization on a new company business plan. For a lot of staff, it may be a relief, because they may have expected something like this for a while. They will see now that finally somebody is taking control of the situation. Keeping staff informed during a difficult situation and keeping them involved in the process to find a way forward has, in my experience, helped to reassure people and to motivate them to participate in hands-on efforts.

Involve the works council or form an employee representative group. The local HR department must play an important role in this as well. Form working groups to discuss the different scenarios and possible action plans. Follow the laws and applicable regulations of the country.

Talk with head office (part of the business plan) about the costs that will be incurred in relation to the number of planned redundancies. There are alternatives such as early retirement, or a bonus for voluntarily leaving the company. There are many more ways to help make it attractive for some people to leave or even start their own company. Another idea could be to let your employees take over a part of the operation by way of outsourcing, and then your company can continue to help them in their new business start up. In most situations, it will be a mix of the above ideas to bring the costs and head count down. Outside local consultants are often needed to follow the right procedures and help you in your contacts with, for example, labour unions. In spite of the bad news of redundancies and a shrinking of the workforce, you will meet with an understanding and even respect, if you show that you care and are fair and eschew politics.

It is a difficult phase in the company's history for the employees and also for you. Do it professionally. That is also what your boss expects from you. Do not forget to prepare yourself for media and TV attention when the reorganization is announced. Train yourself and take care that there is only one capable person in your management team who handles the press (especially, if you do not speak the local language). That can be a company lawyer or Financial manager. In all these matters, you can normally rely on assistance from head office, HR, and the finance, legal and PR departments.

After all these preparations, and emotional, time-consuming actions, you must not forget the remaining workforce. This is the group of people that you will be relying heavily on to help in building a new future and executing the new strategy as part of the business plan. It won't be easy after all the difficulties of the reorganization, to get them focused again and motivated on the challenges that lie ahead. It will be difficult, as well, for them to say goodbye to their colleagues who left. Here you and your management team need to pay very close attention to getting things done and involving all remaining workers in the plans which are needed to make the company healthy again. Take the lead, set examples by energizing the workforce behind new goals and new ways of working. Be visible on the floor and give assistance; and then, let your management team gradually take over your role.

Accept that mistakes may be made initially by staff members in their new positions and roles. Discuss any issues openly and create fun and a fresh motivation wherever possible. Take your staff out and involve them in special activities. For instance, involve all of them, including administrative, production, and engineering staff, in a regional or national sales exhibition of the products you produce and/or sell. Have them visit and participate in these exhibition days. It creates a completely new atmosphere! Be creative and find new ways to bring a new culture into the re-organized company.

1.15   What is your role as general manager?

That is a good question. The answer is that it depends upon the situation in the company you manage as general manager. As soon as the company business plan is accepted, you need to make your own plan on how to execute it. Ask yourself *Who am I?* and *What can I handle and how shall I do it?* Think about what type of general manager you want to be and how you want to act. Do you want to have an open door policy, or perhaps make an early morning appearance and be first in office? Show interest in local community life and, perhaps discuss local sporting events with your staff. Also, look at whether you can benefit from your earlier (similar) experiences and consider what went well and what went wrong. It is a difficult process for which only you can prepare. There is no clear advice or rule that can be given as to how to act, and in which role, because this depends on you and the local situation.

It is important that you have relevant life experiences, and that you know yourself and your communication skills. It is not possible to describe in this book what role you should take. You may find it helpful to discuss the right role with a consultant or perhaps counsellor. Supported by the business plan, you can announce yourself as, and act in the role of, leader, the driver of change and necessary action. This is a role which is normally accepted in Western European countries. If you think the local Management Team and staff can drive the change themselves, then you can take on a support function, or what you might call, the role of coach. In another case, depending on the local culture and habits, you may have to take on a role as a "dictator" for a limited time. Sometimes this is needed when people are not moving ahead and everybody has their own opinion as to how things should be done. You make all decisions, whether there is opposition or not; and by acting in this way, changes will be implemented to your specifications. You may find yourself isolated for many months because you have made yourself unpopular, but you have the vision and conviction that this is the right way of turning the company around. It will always work out in the manner you drive it, because of your energy, will power and conviction. People will begin to join you and support you later on. Even the critics will admit afterward that it was the right direction for the company.

Case Three: Your role as a general manager and refusing orders!

As general manager you should know your organization or company's status completely including all its strengths and weaknesses. I had an experience at one organization where we took in a big order. Unfortunately, this was not handled well because our internal organization was not prepared enough to make it a financial success. Upon investigation, a number of issues were discovered such as, an internal misunderstanding, a lack of coordination, late deliveries, wrong pricing, and quality problems. This was not good, but fortunately, we learned from it. As we were in the process of improving our organization, we suddenly found we could obtain another, more or less similar, order. I refused this one and a lot of my employees could not understand why; but I did not want a repeat of the same problems, including further financial loss. We were simply not yet prepared. We needed more time to get it right. In conclusion, it is important to show leadership even if not everybody will agree with you. You are doing it for the good of the company and its workers.

1.16 General Manager and Human Resources

In this book I describe my experiences and the relations between the general manager and the HR department, in its role of giving service and support to enable the company to reach its goals. In my experience, in fairly large companies a local HR department is needed. But of course, in small organizations and companies where there is no full time HR function, these HR roles have to be handled partly by the financial manager and the general manager. Also the management team can play a role. Sometimes the cooperation of an external lawyer is necessary. Conclusion: the role of the general manager in such situations is also related to HR issues like absences, holidays, issuing guidelines, etc.

CASE FOUR: HOW A WRONG SET UP CAN CREATE UNREST AND STRIKES

In one company, management created different legal structures with different companies for production, sales and services. These legal companies were in the same neighbourhood. In addition, labour relations were inharmonious. As well, salaries differed between the various companies. The result of all this was conflict, the development of strong labour unions and discontent. In some cases, short strikes resulted. When the new general manager arrived, he had to focus on the legal structures. He and his management team investigated not only the legal problems, but also the reasons behind why this legal set up was in place. They needed to determine if it was still a good solution for the business. The HR department played a big role in investigating and later, integrating the conditions of the employees in the different companies. Unrest harmed the overall company and their results.

1.17   How do you handle your own departure?

You handle it in the same way as I described in **1.2**, **"How do you handle the takeover period?** Make it short – one to two weeks maximum. If they call you a hero or are very silent (and maybe happy) when you leave, it is all relative. It is nice to look back and acknowledge that you have achieved something important with your team. Together you gave the company new organization, new energy, pride, drive and a secured future.

As soon as it is known that your successor has been appointed, you immediately become secondary because the focus will be on the new boss. That is human and understandable. You must be able to handle that. Sometimes that may not be easy, because you have an emotional attachment to the company and its employees. That is why you should make your departure brief. I also advise not to return for a visit too soon after your departure. That would make it difficult for your successor. Let him or her handle things the way they want and hope that they will be successful. You have played your role well and after you leave, a new person comes in to introduce a new phase, a new strategy, another style. A different kind of person has to bring the company another step further. You can only hope that the time and energy you have given to the company were not in vain; and due to your efforts, things will go better with the company after you leave. If that is not the case, then the person at the top has a problem.

SECTION 2 –
SITUATIONS I HAVE
EXPERIENCED

2.0 CULTURAL ASPECTS IN YOUR POSITION AS GENERAL MANAGER IN A COMPANY/ ORGANIZATION

Much of your success will depend on how you cope and come to understand cultural aspects of a company in a certain country. To understand the company culture is one of the conditions of success; but also, when you visit your customers or suppliers, you must know the background and some of the history of these companies. For example:

- Is it a family company?

- What is its ethnic background?

- Are there questions of religion?

- Are there tribe-related issues?

- In which part of the country is the company based?

- Is the company/owner related to government or not?

- Is it a noble/aristocratic family?

- Does the owner have an academic background or not at all? Is he a self-made man?

- Are there any customer related issues?

- How does a customer prefer to handle negotiations? Does he or she prefer a long negotiation process, including dinners and discount negotiations, or a short one with only a final price?

- How do you present your business card? What kind of procedure do you have to learn to do it right?

- Is your own company a reflection of the country's religion and ethnic diversity? Is it balanced? This is important in some countries.

In the last example, your own HR department can be of much help. Religion and ethnic diversity have to be part of the selection criteria. What action would you take to avoid internal conflicts or criticism within a company which has an unbalanced ethnic or religious representation? In some countries these questions are not the issue and not important, but in other countries they are.

In Eastern European countries, after the fall of the Soviet Union, I experienced a way of doing business which consisted of having a lot of dinners with a lot of vodka drinking, saunas and entertainment. After, or during all of these activities the deal was made. You got the order because the customer liked you and not only because of the price. Nowadays, most of this way of doing business has disappeared, but elements of this culture still exist. Be prepared.

Another example, and one that for many Western Europeans is not an easy custom, is the habit of men kissing each other when they have a good business relationship and meet up. This custom is indigenous especially to Russia, the Ukraine, and Central Asia.

In a number of countries, a handshake to all employees each morning before work begins, or when you first meet each other during work, is a normal custom. I experienced that in Russia and Indonesia. Exchanging handshakes with workers, engineers, project managers, administrative staff, supervisors and managers is a good way to feel the temperature within the company. During that ceremony people can ask you questions or have comments.

Dealing with all these cultural sensitivities is important. You have to be yourself, but also adapt. Adjust yourself to the circumstances and the cultural aspects of the country, region and your customers and suppliers. Multinational customers often have a common general approach towards suppliers, but also here you must understand where the person you deal with is coming from. Good preparation for a customer visit is essential. Do your homework!

The following illustrates a bad example of what I have been trying to explain. During my Indonesian time, I attended a reception in the residence of a foreign embassy and the female ambassador had also invited a minister of the government, who was male. The minister had his speech, after which, the ambassador thanked His Excellency for his speech and attempted to give him a handshake, which was refused. This did not show good preparation, because in a Muslim country like Indonesia, a woman should not offer to shake hands with a Muslim man (unless he agrees). She should have checked that before! It was unfortunate that everyone in attendance witnessed this blunder.

2.1 Alcohol and drugs (including prescription drugs and stimulants)

In each organization you find alcohol and drug abuse. This includes your company! It is a reality that cannot be ignored, and as general manager, you have to have control and awareness of the situation. Even in a country like Indonesia, with a Muslim majority, you can find alcohol abuse. In a lot of countries, especially in Southern Europe, it is a custom to drink wine during lunch. A normal consumption of alcohol and the use of drugs given on a doctor's prescription can be accepted. But nowadays, alcohol is no longer accepted in factories or offices in working time. Even the use of prescription drugs can have an effect on an employee's concentration. The company's health organization, HR department and the responsible supervisor or manager should be aware of this.

The real problem lies in abuse of these substances. An HR department, together with the company's health organization, if there is one, have important roles to play.

Awareness normally begins with rumours between colleagues, which then spread through the company. The manager of the department concerned must be informed and be involved in the settlement of the problem. In some situations the manager can solve it by him- or herself; otherwise HR can be of assistance. In any case, HR has to advise management, ensuring the validity of any rumours, and together with the manager of the department, decide how to proceed.

It is difficult to be proactive in these cases. A good company policy and company culture can help to avoid these situations; but a lot of substance abuse problems can be caused by private circumstances such as, divorce, the illness of a child, or financial problems. Regional or central HR cannot provide support here because they are too far away; and as it is a local issue, it should be sorted out and dealt with by local HR.

Serious accidents can occur because of abuse, bringing danger not only to the person using drugs or alcohol, but also to their colleagues in the working environment. Unfortunately, I have experienced some situations, as described below:

- A male employee, who was working a good deal of overtime for a few weeks, used energizers during work to stay alert. He went home after work, took energizers again, played some badminton with his daughter; and unfortunately, when he returned home, he suffered a fatal heart attack.

- An employee was suspected of using drugs during working hours. Rumours started in the company; he was warned to stop and offered help. Unfortunately, he continued and lost his job.

- In a company that employed 1,000 people, there was notorious abuse of alcohol during work hours. We had a medical health organization consisting of two doctors and three nurses and we were still not able to take control of the situation. We discussed this problem with those involved and warned them that this would not be tolerated. We also offered help and support. In the end, unfortunately, most of them were dismissed because of continuing alcohol use and their affected behaviour during work. It is difficult to imagine what a problem that must have been to the families at home.

- Do not underestimate the amount of people in your company who use too many prescription drugs to control stress, or for other reasons. A local HR department has a clear task here, together with the departmental manager, to follow up on rumours for the sake of the company and their workers. You must endeavour to control these situations! Offer support, medical advice or social work, if needed. As general manager, your task is also to care and be fair. In this case, fair means that you cannot tolerate a weak approach in these situations. You have to protect the company and its employees!

2.2 Calamities and accidents

You might have to deal with earthquakes, floods, diseases, riots, strikes or other social unrest in any country where the company is based.

- Normally, companies have a kind of organization like an ERT (Emergency Response Team) and a fire brigade, consisting of volunteers from the company's staff who are trained and have the equipment to act in case of floods, earthquakes and fire. Get to know them because, when needed, they do an enormously important job. Invest in equipment, if needed. It is also greatly appreciated by the families when help is urgently needed, like distributing food and drinking water in case of floods. It supports the company culture and creates a very strong bond between all employees. Everybody helps each other!

- Diseases such as dengue fever or other local sicknesses can be controlled by good preventive action from your medical team or outside medical services.

- In the case of riots, you can have support from embassies who can give you daily updates on the situation. There are special organizations and companies who can give all kinds of advice, or even organize an evacuation, if needed. Often, your head office is also equipped with an organization that can support you with evacuation or can advise you about the steps you and your family need to take.

- Strikes in your company or on the industrial estate where your company is based, need 100% of your attention and a lot of support from your HR department. If the company itself is affected, then you, your management team and the HR department must solve the problem. Normally, you can avoid strikes if you have a good relationship with a works council or workers' representative group, along with a functioning local HR department.

I experienced a strike when our outsourced workers were not paid by the outsourcing company, in spite of all the promises that had been made. They stopped working and came to my office! We promised to solve the problem immediately and, thanks to the staff in our financial department (they worked the whole night to prepare payments), we managed to give all workers on that shift an advance the same night.

- Strikes on an industrial estate, where the company is based, can affect your company and cause problems. The workers from other companies may ask your workers to show solidarity. When you have a good working climate, a good salary system, and a good atmosphere, you can keep things under control, together with the help of HR and the workers' representatives, so it will not harm your company. It could temporarily create some tension, but what you have invested in the company's culture will pay off during such critical moments.

Accidents

- Each company, I assume, has some type of first aid-trained organization and a health committee to discuss, register and analyze accidents or the frequency of sickness absence in departments. As general manager, you must participate in these meetings which are often held on a monthly basis. It would be wrong to consider these meetings as unimportant, because you might have better things to do with your time. By participating, you show your commitment and the employees see and feel that you really care about the work this committee is doing. The health of your employees during working time is a very important responsibility.

Sometimes I would have nightmares where I would be dreaming of a deadly accident occurring in the workshop.

An accident can happen, for instance, when people are tired due to working too much overtime. Please control overtime rigorously! A sick person, or a person using drugs or energizers, as an example, may be the source of an accident. In the end, you, as general manager, are responsible. In the worst case scenario, you could be prosecuted and go to jail if something very serious happened.

- Frequent safety drills are needed. Appoint a safety officer, with the authority to stop work in case an unsafe situation is occurring. It does not have to be a full time person. It could be, for instance, a maintenance manager or somebody from their department who can combine this position with their own work. It depends, of course, on the type of work or industry you are in; but even if you only have engineers or sales and installation personnel working in your company, you need to pay attention to safety. This is especially so when installation work is taking place at the customer's site. Also, the customer will expect safe behaviour from installation companies.

- Car accidents can happen, and can sometimes be deadly. For instance, employees driving hundreds of kilometres at night in treacherous conditions, or a drunken driver causing injury to your employee or damaging their vehicle. Tragic accidents can cause enormous suffering for the families. Care about safety. Make sure your employees know to stop driving before they become tired and that they take rest breaks or even check into a hotel.

- Accidents in your operation have to be handled locally. It has been my experience that with serious accidents, a delegation from head office also shows its sympathy, which is of course, very much appreciated. But local management has to settle the compensation and handle the details. In a few cases, when head office stepped in and dealt with it, there were very negative results. This happened because they did not understand the local culture. Their good intentions went wrong, which culminated in a court case. Sadly, the people got the idea that much more money could be paid by the company.

Pay attention and do as much as possible to avoid these tragedies. If it happens, take care that there is a good insurance policy and a good backup plan is ready.

2.3   Obstruction and sabotage

Unfortunately these situations happen. Why? Well, you might think it would be because of laziness or lack of interest in the job. Do employees try to push the boundaries? Has dissatisfaction culminated into hate? No attention for the problems of workers? Perhaps there is neglect by management. People who cause these problems are aware that they are taking chances with their own job; but they do not care that it could be lost. They simply want to harm the company.

There are actually a number of reasons why this happens. You, your management team and your local HR department must be aware that it could happen. Due to staff solidarity, it is very difficult to get the name of the guilty person. In my opinion, the only way to stop or avoid this kind of behaviour altogether, is to have an awareness of the company's culture of motivation and taking away or paying attention to employee complaints. Take steps to have meetings with all employees that focus on the positive, that celebrate something. It is important to have fun and involve employees in sharing the company's successes. In the end, it is the employees who create the success, not you. In that way you also create a kind of "social control" between the employees which helps them to feel they do not want to harm the company, as it will harm all of them.

Below are a few examples of situations that I have experienced.

- A person working in the quality control department had a task to fill in the result of batches he had to check and control during his shift. However, instead he filled in fake results even before he started his shift. That deception went unnoticed until a batch was wrong and complaints came from the market. I was 26 years old and it was my first job in HR. Unfortunately, I had no choice but to dismiss this person. This person happened to be elderly. When I spoke to him, he fainted. A nurse came and helped him. I offered to take him home, but he was angry and refused. However, I followed him by car until I was sure he arrived home safely. But that was not the end of the matter!

  A few months later, I met him in a park in the city and asked him how he was doing. He smelled of alcohol and said that everything was okay. I investigated and found out that he had not told his wife and family that he had been dismissed. Every day he left home at what would have been his normal time and came home at the normal time. In the meantime, he passed his time in parks and cafes. It was a tragic story. Sometime later, a social work organization that was contacted tried to help him.

- In another situation, we discovered that mistakes were made deliberately within a drawing and in the assembly of a machine. In both cases this resulted in a claim. Since it could have been done collectively, how would you go about trying to find the person? The only way would be by devoting a lot of attention to improving staff morale and motivation in order to avoid too much damage.

- Another time, a manager financed a private situation with company money. This was obviously not allowed nor did he have the authority to allow it to occur. Another case came up where a person stole money from the company. All cases of this type have to be handled fairly, but strictly. Most international companies have compliance rules and directives to handle such situations. If your staff notices that you do not take action, you are in a bad situation. However, keep your actions clear – only one person committed a criminal act, therefore, do not punish the whole company for it as if you do not trust anybody anymore! This will result in the opposite reaction from the one you want. Again, handle such situations with tact and care but be fair. Employees will observe and notice how you react. Based on the directives of your head office, you must inform and notify the respective department or an auditing group. Make a report of your actions because this is your responsibility, not that of head office.

These situations are not an easy part of being a general manager, but the way you solve them and the respect you receive later on when it has all gone well, will help you to establish employee trust and confidence in the management of the company. That will help you with many more of the objectives you have set!

2.4   Strategy and your departments

As general manager in an operation, you are working very much "hands on", as you have read in the previous cases and situations. But, of course, there is also an important element of strategic thinking needed. You do not constantly have to deal with operations. It is not an easy task to develop a strategy and make it part of the company's business plan. Moreover, to get such a plan accepted by your management team, your employees and your bosses will need time. This requires endurance, good planning and a strategy to follow so that your plan gets accepted in the end. There is, more than likely, an urgency and need for radical change in the company and you are the one who has the vision and must lead the process. (If you involve all department managers and the management team, you will never achieve a radical change in the company's direction since everybody is protecting his or her own interests).

So much depends on the situation. In my experience, during the difficult assignments I carried out, I initiated the changes and was, therefore, in most cases, the driver of the process. Timing, in general, is important when it is related to budget reviews, when changes in the company are needed or when new developments and information from head office are announced. It all needs careful planning and a step-by-step approach to get your plans, and often financing requirements or investments, accepted. You have to discuss that with your superior;

and, if they are in support of your plans, then you jointly plan for the right approach. When your business plan is finally accepted, you can concentrate on the implementation.

Your business plan now becomes the company's business plan. From time to time, at least once a year, or even better, twice a year, you have to discuss the company's business plan with your superior, your management team and employee representatives based on the progress you have achieved. Discuss any adjustments you might want to suggest, speeding up and improving even further the company's situation. It is an ongoing process with an end result of a re-energized and profitable company.

An operational company can have three basic economic and financial formats.

A) Operating as a "back office" company which is developing and manufacturing goods and also supporting the sales activities, but which is not responsible for the final sales and engineering result.

B) Operating as a "front office" company, selling manufactured (by the "back office") products in a country or region. This consists of a sales organization involved in the engineering, project management, installation and after sales.

C) Or, operating as both "front" and "back office", an integrated company that covers all activities.

I have managed and worked in all three organizational formats.

I will explain some of my experiences within the departments of finance and IT, sales, HR, production, and supply management.

Finance and IT

Finance and IT is one of the most important departments in a company and will have a good control of the financial flow. In other words, it will have control of the receivables and liabilities. The final bottom line result is what it is all about. You have more or less daily contact with the financial manager or director. Together, you operate as a small team who control the invoices and sales figures, to mention a few. It is essential to follow the financial development of the turnaround task you have in front of you. Trust between you and the responsible financial manager is crucial toward making this team work. In some assignments, I was not lucky in finding the right financial team member. Later on, this caused me a lot of problems and surprises. You cannot be 100% sure of success when working on a program of change if your financial colleagues are not supportive or if they do not have the necessary competence and capabilities. It is crucial to have the right person and have a good chemistry between you and the responsible financial team member. Fortunately, in my last few assignments, I had a good working relationship which made the work much easier and less stressful to know that this part (the finances and related administration) was under control. As well, you should be a part of any contact with auditors and the discussions about the yearly auditing report.

Also follow the development of the organization of the finance department to ensure that it is not growing too fast in staff. This is especially important nowadays because a lot of IT systems, introduced by central office, make it easier to get a good and quick financial overview, and extra staff is often not necessary.

Financial reporting to head office should be done correctly and on time. Just follow it from time to time and have contact with the finance department within head office to check that they are satisfied with the format and content of your company reporting. It is also important that you do the necessary budgetary work and investment preparation in conjunction with the management team. The financial responsible has a crucial task in collecting all data and discussing it thoroughly with you as the general manager and with the management team. After that, it's down to a balanced presentation to your superior. This will ensure that you are well prepared when you have to present it as part of the yearly budget process. Priorities have to be set and the general manager's role is that of the initiator in getting it right and done on time, as well as in accordance with an existing business plan or based on new developments. The financial manager or director is, in my opinion, more than a person collecting figures and reporting. He or she should also be involved in the sales process. In time, as part of the sales process, he or she should check the financial background of new customers. As well, payment arrangements should be discussed with the responsible sales person in relation to the company's cash flow situation. This should not be decided by the sales department on its own. The financial manager can also be part of a price negotiation in order to assist sales. These are all very useful contributions, which makes the negotiation more successful, and in the end, contributes to the success of the company. It also creates a better team. Often, finance is working in isolation within a management team. You avoid that with this approach; and you let the financial manager grow in his abilities so much so that he may become a candidate to replace you!

The IT department, as a specialized support function (for instance, in installing up-to-date software and other IT developments), can be a good contributor because it supports company efficiency and goals. But that is, unfortunately, not always the case. Often, if it is a centralized organization, decisions are sometimes forced upon you as general manager, which does not help you locally. The service is limited to the overall organization and not to your specific company situation. It does not need to be tailor-made, but some flexibility is needed to have better success. This can be done by arranging solutions for typical situations which exist due to local laws, local customs and tax regulations. It is often possible to easily solve this by specific programming. As general manager, you have to use your creativity and sometimes diplomacy to handle this in the best way for the company. You develop your own internal solutions to solve issues, and at the same time, avoid a problem with head office.

Sales

A very interesting department and one I very much enjoyed dealing with, was the sales department. I enjoyed, when necessary, assisting sales people in their job. Sales people working with engineering people in preparing quotations and following up the commercial contacts are sometimes in need of help. Occasionally, some customers, often family companies, want to do the final negotiations with the big boss present.

I also enjoyed working with the sales team on final margins and price limits, especially when it was based on good preparation. Often, it can be a lot like playing poker which can be good for both sides as long as the customer also prefers this negotiation process. It is very rewarding when you and your sales team manage to get the order. Multinational companies often have a different approach. They ask a limited number of selected suppliers to quote; and they decide who to give the order to, based on the final quote. As supplier, you must be free to decide to quote or not; although, it is not always appreciated if you decide not to quote. Also central marketing, who are responsible for international key accounts, always want you to quote even if the margin is rather low. Internal discussions may follow to solve that problem. In one case, I refused to quote for an order with an international customer as we had previously quoted twice; and we felt we were being used as a "price breaker", with the client's sole aim being to obtain a reduced offer from a competitor. So we lost twice to the same competitor. When they invited us a third time (according to their procedure, they were required to invite a certain number of suppliers for quotations and we were needed to fulfil that requirement), I decided to refuse because it cost our company a lot of time and money to prepare another quotation which, quite likely, would have had no result. The customer became very angry and wanted to force me to quote. My opinion was that we must be free to quote or not. It turned out that he contacted head office and my superior with the complaint that "a guy in that country refused to quote", which he could not accept. My superior called me and I explained that we did not want to be used again for bargaining purposes only because I was aware that they had a long and good relationship with our competitor. My superior accepted my argument. But many years later, this person, when he again met my superior, recalled the situation and was still complaining about "that guy" (me) who refused to quote. So you see, there are a number of ways you can make your mark!

Sales is a very interesting department, with hardworking people; but occasionally, they believe they are the most important people in the company since it is them who seem to generate the income. That is, of course, not the case. The sales team has the contact with the (potential) customers and needs the general manager to support them in their work, even when they try out new, creative commercial approaches. It is all based on teamwork. Together, with engineering, production, quality and installation, we create the sales and obtain the orders. More cooperation with other departments is necessary and the focus has to be on working together. The sales department remains responsible for the order they take in, even with an appointed manager handling the project. The customer made the deal with them, so in case there are problems, sales must be responsible and follow the work in project meetings. It is in their interest to successfully complete the order and to obtain an eventual new order from the customer. The project must go smoothly. Promises made verbally by sales people may, at times, be very difficult for a responsible project manager to fulfil. Therefore, all meetings between sales people and customers need to be followed up with a short report of what was discussed and promised. This avoids confusion later.

Human Resources

In my book, published in February 2013, about human resources and entitled, *Human Resources in Crisis*, I write about the importance of having a local HR department, the importance of a company culture and how to maintain or create such a culture in a company. I also write about what HR can do and how they can contribute to the success of the company as a real, active and creative partner, having a focus on the human capital of the company. In the past, they may have taken on the role of cost controller or administrator by sitting behind their computers all day working "by the book" handed down from central office. These days, though, HR needs to pay attention to the relationships between people, motivation, quality awareness, fun in work and creating, together with other departments, an atmosphere of professionalism, pride and quality. In short, a company culture that works daily toward the improvement of the organization. HR needs to be open to new developments and new IT systems, as long as they support the working atmosphere and relationships between employees. By doing that, the employees' contribution to the positive results in a company increases. It creates trust and trust is built on performance.

A professional HR department begins with what is called their "ABC work". This consists of recruitment, selection, training, and induction of employees. As well, they have to work on organizational development, employee relations, conflicts and mediation and health and safety issues. Salary systems and promotion policies bring stability to a company, which can deliver quality when employees are motivated. Contact with an HR department located in a central or head office can provide professional service in specialized subjects such as, pension systems and job evaluation procedures; and this help is very much appreciated. Discuss and contribute together with head office new ideas or systems, but before new systems are introduced, check these new ideas within your local company to avoid problems and failures afterwards.

The above actions reflect the initiatives needed to develop and create a unique company culture. The general manager has an important role to play here by continually setting examples. It starts with focussing on motivational activities such as fun in work, job rotation, training and education. It also demonstrates the sum of the company's culture and acknowledges unwritten feelings, relationships, and the company's inner workings and its workers.

Production

Production is one of the most difficult departments to manage. One of the reasons for this is that production is where everything that has been agreed, promised and designed comes together. Initially by sales; then engineering gets involved; then supply management and purchasing join in to take care the ordered product comes in time. After that, the products have to be produced and delivered in top quality and within the agreed time. It requires a world class manufacturing output. So the production department is under constant stress. Much of this stress must be avoided to the extent possible so it does not affect quality. To avoid at least some problems in the production process, a suggestion could be that the production manager or director discusses the terms of delivery with the sales manager, project manager and the supply chain at the time a quotation is being prepared for the customer. Good production planning, cost control, quality awareness, and contacts regarding delivery of materials with warehouse and purchasing all help to avoid delays. Interruptions in the process create costs, demotivation of employees and dissatisfaction in clients. Management of people by team leaders, supervisors and managers is demanding because the focus on employee-related aspects is often not part of their training. The HR department can lend support here by advising the organization in production. It is difficult to get it right.

Being a production manager or director is a very demanding, but interesting and rewarding job, as long as you can see progress. Teamwork within a management team is needed to discuss any problems in the order flow. Production needs several things to work in sync in order to have orders coming in (factory in full capacity), such as needing the investments to bring costs down (finance), delivery of the material at the right time (warehouse and purchasing = supply chain), the right level of quality (quality control) with packaging and shipping done correctly (supply chain). Add to all this good management and avoiding labour disputes (HR), and it all comes together in the final product. So the sales department can be optimistic about getting the next order thanks to the right delivery and quality. Everyone knows it takes hard work to produce an ideal outcome. The people responsible for managing the entire production process need to have full support.

Supply management

Supply management is the new word for the old purchasing, warehouse, and distribution departments. This new name is reflective of all the activities and services previously covered by all three of the old departments. As a result, a lot of new ideas and activities have started and are being developed by this new department, often centrally organized. Sometimes with a little too much reporting and administrative procedures and too many centralized directives which, again, as in other departments too, are not giving services to the operating companies but are often felt as hazards. That is a pity and then the process does not work in an optimized way.

You cannot run a supply management department from a central office somewhere far away without considering the unique local culture and situation. For instance, in some countries the local supplier needs help in getting his quality to the same level as the receiving company. A lot of work and support has to be undertaken to get that right. If you do not allow that to be done, then it will be no surprise when the outcome is not good. What is good and contributes to the company's favourable results, are the global multinational suppliers' contracts, which fix, in a certain context, the price. In this way, you avoid big price differences in each country and that helps with your competitive position. Although not all price agreements work as they should, it is a big improvement. Still, the local company needs to have the freedom to select other suppliers locally if their services are better, or when the price and quality is equal to or better than the global contract. If that is permitted and agreed upon, it will ensure that the supply management department is a real contributor to the company's success.

There is a tendency to control all supply management activities centrally and also to develop direct reporting lines to the central supply management office. Also you will see that some companies are trying to develop a centrally controlled HR department. If you have to manage an operation as managing director or general manager, and it is your responsibility to deliver financial results such as a positive operating result, then *all* management team members and their respective departments have to report to you. You are not a "puppet-on-a-string", where the final decisions are made somewhere out of your control and responsibility. Of course, there are lines of reporting to central or head office that must be followed by the different departments. I suggest following these lines in the way established by the finance manager or director. He or she is part of the management team and reports to the managing director or general manager, but also works with some financial departments in head office.

2.5   A classic quality problem

I want to close this chapter with a classic quality problem. It is a problem often discussed in many companies, including my former companies, and requires a strong will, determination and organization to really solve it.

The problem seems to be that commonly, companies are not able to make use of the enormous experiences of the installation people, service engineers and technicians, who work in the field, at the customers' sites. They see and hear a lot about competitors' products, which may be much better or worse than ours and closer to the clients' expectations. For instance, how the goods arrived and how they were packed. They experienced the initial use and functioning of the product and the attitude of (foreign) service engineers. There may have been many complaints about the execution of the work and about deliveries that may have gone wrong. This is all valuable information which can be learnt from, but it is not necessarily used to its advantage. There is not sufficient feedback. Communication and follow-up (feedback) are needed between the people in the field (installation) on one side, and the designers, developers and producers on the other. Learning from mistakes and being able to change, is very important. Yet, there often is no interest and no real action is taken to solve these problems for next time. So there is, of course, no or little improvement.

Let the engineers, who design the equipment and deliver solutions, visit the customer and see on site that the solutions which they create may, in practice and at times, be overly complicated and not suitable. Why not have engineers or production workers visit or work as an apprentice on a customer's site to learn how difficult it is to install the equipment (produced and engineered by their colleagues) and complete the start-up. Be active in getting feedback from customers and follow the needed or suggested improvements. It can work to your advantage in the next project with this customer if you have solved the problems they mentioned. Do you know of a company or organization that has finally gotten all these communication problems and related frustrations solved and got things better organized? Do you know of any company who has improved their organization, learned from their mistakes and would not let it happen again? Such a new approach would take advantage of good and adequate feedback and implement immediate corrections in the organization.

It will help the company a lot and especially the sales, production, after sales, engineering and quality control departments. I was not able to solve all of these problems in my forty years of work. But I hope and expect that you, as responsible general manager, pay attention to this problem and work toward a solution. Then it will be time for *you* to write a book filled with your solutions and experiences.

SUMMARY

As I pointed out throughout this book, it contains some autobiographical elements. I mentioned some real cases which I experienced to make my arguments more clear and illustrative. Of course, I could not answer all "1001" questions; but I hope that the questions I did raise in this book and the situations I described may have answered a lot of your questions or at least conveyed to you the opinion of a person with 40 years' experience. It is up to you to decide. I hope that, at least, it provides you with something to think about or to discuss. If that is the case, then this small book has fulfilled its purpose

Now we come to the last question of the "1001".

You might ask me, *Rudolf, you answered many questions, but how do you describe yourself as manager?* My answer to that will always be, *Good question*! But seriously, two countries I worked in, referred to me as coach and boss (who knows what they called me behind my back). My superior at the time sarcastically called me "the most democratic leader" he'd ever met. I responded that I learned from him.

Not all my general manager periods and assignments were a success business-wise; but in spite of all the hard work by everyone, I enjoyed it. At least we moved the companies forward.

Did I experience failure as well? Yes. In one of my assignments managing a "back office" company, which had made a loss for many years, we planned a big reorganization, including downsizing based on a new business plan and with the support of head office. A lot of negotiations followed with unions, workers' representatives and all employees because everybody understood that something had to be done. It took us a few years and when this process came to an end, we had achieved our objectives, which were creating a smaller company set up that was better equipped and more flexible. But, of course, we needed orders (sales). As a "back office" company we depended, to a great extent, on the order intake from the "front office" companies who were selling our products. Unfortunately, our business was in an industrial cycle of less investment at that time and fewer orders came in. There were not even enough orders for a scaled-down organizational set up. So, in spite of our "slimming down", we still could not solve our bottom line result, to deliver black figures.

It was, however, a great learning experience. A general manager develops into a leader through time and circumstance. During the most difficult period of leadership, even one that might involve failure, you do your best. Then you deserve, because of all the creativity and effort you put in, at least the recognition of these efforts. But it is not always understood correctly by your bosses and head office because technically, your score is low and your result is not viewed as good. Paradoxically, when you do less hard work, but the business climate is favourable, showing success and good results, you get compliments and a good bonus. Because the time was right and the country was booming, the good results and success came more or less by themselves. That's life.

As you have no doubt read in the newspapers and followed on TV, not everyone is treated in this manner. There are captains of industry and CEOs responsible for millions or even billions of USD/Euro losses in the companies they manage and yet, they still receive a whopping bonus for their "performance". That is also life.

Rudolf Hartong

ABOUT THE AUTHOR

Rudolf Hartong was born 1947 and worked for forty years in human resources and general management positions. Both his education and background are in human resources. He actively worked in human resources for twenty-two years, mainly in the Netherlands, Spain, Switzerland, and Sweden. For the remaining eighteen years he worked in operational general management positions as managing director, general manager, and executive vice president in Russia (two assignments). He has also worked in the Netherlands and Indonesia – mostly in turnaround positions: change management and re-engineering of companies.

He has been retired since July 2012, and, in response to numerous requests, is writing down his experiences. Rudolf and his wife now live in Switzerland.

For comments and remarks, you may contact
Rudolf Hartong via email at:
rudolfhartong@yahoo.com

You can follow him on his blog at: www.rudolfhartong.com

www.ingramcontent.com/pod-product-compliance
Lightning Source LLC
Chambersburg PA
CBHW022126170526
45157CB00004B/1770